ECO STEAM

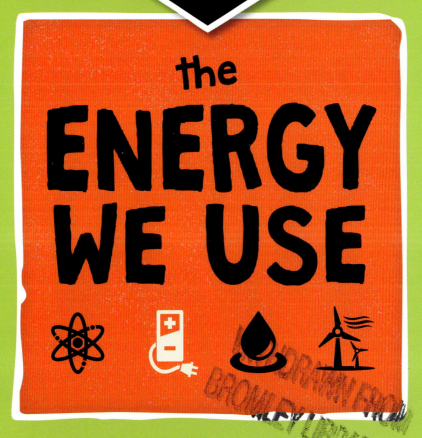

the ENERGY WE USE

GEORGIA AMSON-BRADSHAW

WAYLAND
www.waylandbooks.co.uk

First published in Great Britain in 2018 by Wayland

Produced for Wayland by
White-Thomson Publishing Ltd
www.wtpub.co.uk

Series Editor: Georgia Amson-Bradshaw
Series Designer: Rocket Design (East Anglia) Ltd

ISBN: 978 1 5263 0790 3
10 9 8 7 6 5 4 3 2 1

Wayland
An imprint of
Hachette Children's Group
Part of Hodder & Stoughton
Carmelite House
50 Victoria Embankment
London EC4Y 0DZ

An Hachette UK Company
www.hachette.co.uk
www.hachettechildrens.co.uk

Printed in Dubai

Picture acknowledgements:
Images from Shutterstock.com: Vector 4t, George Rudy 4c, NEGOVURA 4b, Merla 5t, Boutique Isometrique 5c, ProStockStudio 5b, Dmitry Sedakov 6t, Arcansel 6b, Rudmer Zwerver 7t, Jovanovic Dejan 7bl, Vladi333 8t, MC_Noppadol 8b, FloridaStock 9t, Macrovector 9b, hramovnick 11r, Tatiana Stulbo 12t, Puslatronik 12b, ArtMari 13t, justone 16t, wawritto 16b, R. Vickers 17t, Mike Shooter 17c, Drogatnev 17b, metamorworks 18t, nnattalli 18b, Fotokostic 19t, Stockr 19b, petovarga 20t, daulon 20c, brown32 20b, MoonRock 21t, Iconic Bestiary 24, testing 24b, Nina Puankova 25t, Dragon Images 25c, Anticiclo 25b, Cherkas 26t, NEGOVURA 27t, Sirocco 27c, Anton Watman 27b, petovarga 28t, Art Alex 28b, Studio BKK 29t, Romaset 29c, cozyta 32c, Ira Yapanda 32b, mmmx 33t, Oleskova Olha 33b, oorka 34t, Desingua 34b, Olga Shishova 35t, petovarga 35c, Jason Benz Bennee 35b, Tom Grundy 36t, Kit8.net 36l, AlenKadr 37t, SkyPics Studio 37b, zhangyang13576997233 40t, Iterum 41c, TatyanaTVK 42t, ribz 42l, Vector Mine 42r, Oliver Hoffman 43, Macrovector 44t, ProStockStudio 44r, Frederic Legrand -COMEO 44b, CW Craftsman 45t, Sentavio 45b, Julia's Art 46t, Africa Studio 46c, Bukhavets Mikhail 46b

Image from wiki commons: Tennessee Valley Authority 10, NASA 41t

Illustrations by Steve Evans: 15, 23, 31, 39

All design elements from Shutterstock.

CONTENTS

UNDERSTANDING ENERGY

What is energy? The scientific definition is 'the capacity to do work', but what does that mean? Energy is what makes things happen. It makes machines work, and plants grow. It's what birds use to fly and what we use to power our devices. Our ability to harness and control energy is part of what has made humans so successful as a species.

Types of energy

Energy comes in many forms, but they all belong to two main types: kinetic energy and potential energy. Kinetic energy is sometimes called movement energy. It is the sort of energy that moving objects have, such as a bowling ball rolling along the floor. The other kind of energy is potential energy. This is the kind of energy that fuels, such as coal, contain. The energy is stored up, ready to do something.

SPOTLIGHT:

CONSERVATION OF ENERGY

Energy cannot be created or destroyed. It can only be changed from one form to another. Scientists call this fact the 'conservation of energy'. For example, the potential energy in coal is changed into heat and light energy when it is burned.

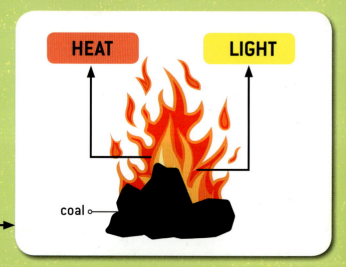

HEAT   LIGHT

coal

Using energy

Humans use different types of energy every day. We eat food, which contains chemical (potential) energy. Our bodies change it into heat energy that keeps our body temperature stable, and kinetic energy as we walk around. We use electrical energy to power our homes, and turn it into light and sound energy through our TVs. We put fuels containing chemical energy into our cars, which ultimately turn it into kinetic energy that moves us around.

A resting human turns energy from food into body heat at a rate of around 80 watts — about the same amount of power as a laptop uses!

Converting energy

Energy is everywhere, but the kind of energy that we are focusing on in this book is the energy that we use to power our homes, factories and transport. Our ability to change or convert energy that is stored as fuel into other types of energy has been essential to our history of technological development. But our reliance on fuels has come at a cost. Read more about this on the next few pages.

Our cars use the energy that is stored in petrol or diesel.

HOW WE USE FUELS

For much of human history, the main type of fuel people used was biomass, such as wood. The ability to start a fire and keep it going with fuel helped our ancestors to keep warm and cook their food. Fire also allowed humans to develop other technologies, such as firing clay to make pottery, and smelting metal into tools.

SPOTLIGHT: BIOMASS

Organic matter such as wood, straw or even animal dung that is burned for fuel is called biomass. 10 per cent of the global energy supply is currently from biomass.

animal dung

wood chips

straw

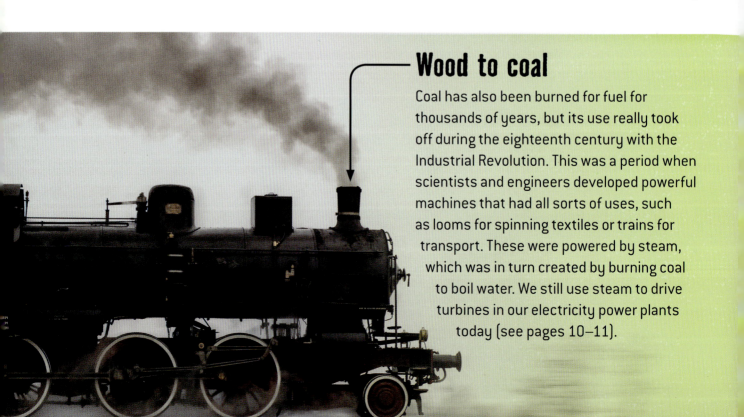

Wood to coal

Coal has also been burned for fuel for thousands of years, but its use really took off during the eighteenth century with the Industrial Revolution. This was a period when scientists and engineers developed powerful machines that had all sorts of uses, such as looms for spinning textiles or trains for transport. These were powered by steam, which was in turn created by burning coal to boil water. We still use steam to drive turbines in our electricity power plants today (see pages 10–11).

Fossil fuels

Coal is a fossil fuel, along with crude oil and natural gas. Fossil fuels are formed from the ancient remains of plants and animals, that were buried deep underground for millions of years. Over time, the extreme heat and pressure underground turned those remains into fossil fuels that contain energy.

Combustion engine

The late nineteenth century saw the development of the internal combustion engine. Instead of heating water, this technology burns fuels such as petrol or diesel directly to drive a machine. As the internal combustion engine weighed less than a steam engine, it allowed the development of vehicles such as cars and aeroplanes.

An 1899 Renault Type C petrol-powered motor car

Global warming

Unfortunately, our heavy dependence on fossil fuels is causing big problems. Burning fossil fuels releases gases into the Earth's atmosphere, which trap heat from the Sun. This is causing the Earth to heat up, and is disrupting global weather patterns – with serious consequences. Read more about this on the next page.

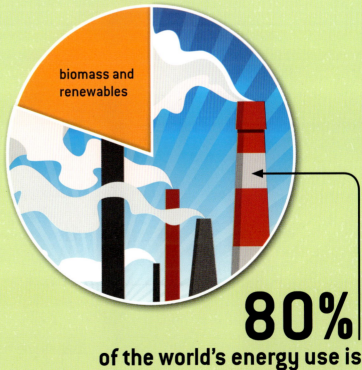

biomass and renewables

80%
of the world's energy use is currently powered by fossil fuels.

CLIMATE CHANGE

Our planet is surrounded by a thin layer of gases, called the atmosphere. It acts like a see-through blanket, protecting us from dangerous radiation from the Sun, while trapping enough of the Sun's warmth to allow life to thrive. But human activity is altering the atmosphere, causing climate change.

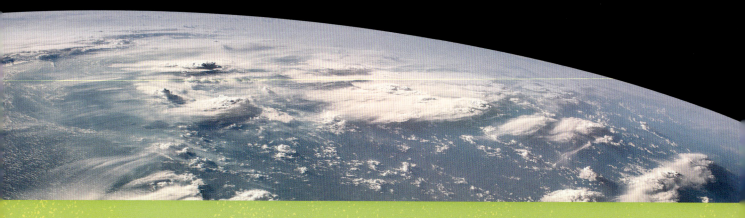

Gases in the atmosphere

Our atmosphere is made of a mixture of gases, mostly nitrogen and oxygen, with small amounts of gases such as carbon dioxide, methane and water vapour. Fossil fuels are made of carbon, and when they are burned, they release carbon dioxide into the air. Over time, the amount of carbon dioxide in the atmosphere has been increasing.

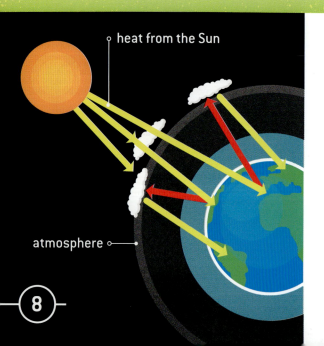

heat from the Sun

atmosphere

The greenhouse effect

Carbon dioxide, along with methane and water vapour, are greenhouse gases, meaning they trap heat from the Sun in the atmosphere – just like a greenhouse. As the amount of greenhouse gases in the atmosphere increases, the overall temperature of the Earth increases too.

Average surface temperatures on Earth could rise between 2°C and 6°C by the end of the twenty-first century.

Melting ice

The increase in global temperatures has effects around the world. Ice at the polar regions melts, causing global sea levels to increase. This can result in flooding, particularly in very low-lying areas such as small islands.

The Arctic could be free of ice by 2040.

Heavy weather

Global warming also affects weather patterns. Because warm air can hold more water vapour than cold air, a warmer atmosphere means more water is stored as clouds. In some areas this causes drought, because the clouds don't reach saturation point and drop the water as rain. In places where it does rain, this can cause flooding, due to all the additional water that clouds are able to carry before finally dropping it. It can also cause more extreme and violent storms, as extra heat in the air or the oceans is a type of energy, and tropical storms are driven by such energy.

Human impacts

Flooding and drought can prevent crops from growing, which can result in famine. Flooding and storms can destroy people's homes, forcing them to move. People being forced to move from their homes in large numbers can cause tension and unrest.

storms

flooding

drought

PRODUCING POWER

The biggest source of greenhouse gases that contribute to climate change is the production of electricity and heat. They come from the burning of fossil fuels in power plants, which convert the chemical energy in coal, oil and gas into electricity and heating for our businesses and homes.

31 per cent of the world's greenhouse gases are released as we burn fossil fuels to generate electricity and heat.

HOW WE GENERATE ELECTRICITY
Traditional power plants work in the following way:

1 Fuel containing chemical energy, such as coal, oil or gas, is burnt in a furnace, creating heat energy. This energy is used to heat pipes containing water, which turns the water into steam.

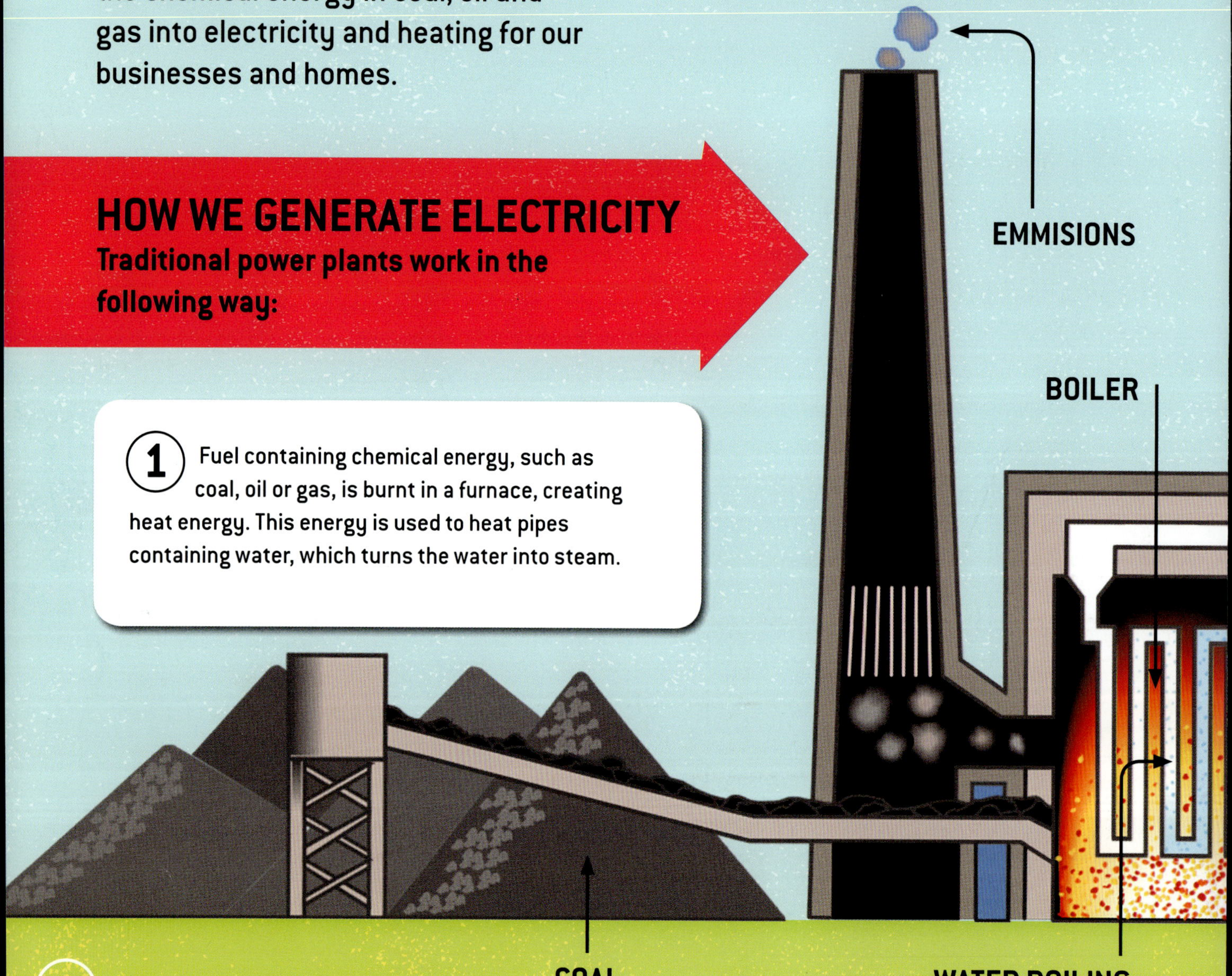

EMMISIONS

BOILER

COAL

WATER BOILING

Surprisingly, the amount of carbon dioxide (CO_2) that is produced from burning a fuel weighs more than the amount of the fuel itself. This is because each carbon atom in the fuel combines with two oxygen atoms in the air to make CO_2 when it burns. Read about this on page 27.

2 The steam is used to spin a turbine, which is like a windmill made of many metal blades. At this stage, the steam's energy is converted into kinetic energy, spinning the turbine very fast. The steam is condensed back into water to be used again.

3 The spinning turbine is linked to a generator. Inside the generator, metal wires are spun past very strong magnets. This creates an electrical current in the wires, converting the kinetic, spinning energy into electrical energy. Electricity then flows out through cables to reach our homes and factories.

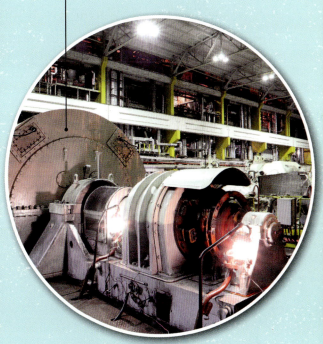

Large generators inside a power plant

STEAM

TURBINE

OUTPUT

GENERATOR

All in the spin

So in a power plant, electricity is generated by spinning metal wires at very high speeds past very strong magnets. Burning fuel to make steam is just one method for creating that spinning movement.

SOLVE IT!
GREEN ENERGY SOURCES

Producing electricity using a generator doesn't have to depend on burning fuel, if alternative ways to create a fast spinning motion can be found. Fortunately, there is plenty of energy available from natural sources that can be harnessed for the task. Can you see how?

WIND

Human beings have used the energy in wind to do work, such as grind corn or power boats, for thousands of years.

Do you know:

▶ **What sort of energy wind contains?**

▶ **What piece of technology can be used to harness it to spin generators?**

EARTH

The centre of the Earth is incredibly hot. In some places around the world, heat from inside the Earth gets quite close to the Earth's surface. In those areas, you don't have to dig too deeply to find very hot rock. Think about how electricity is generated in most power plants:

▶ **How could underground heat be used to drive generators?**

volcanic area

hot magma

WATER

Chemical energy isn't the only kind of potential energy. Another type is gravitational potential energy. When an object or material is held up against the force of gravity, it contains potential energy. Think of a cyclist poised at the top of a hill. As they sit there with the brakes on, they have the 'potential' to start rolling downwards. Releasing the brakes causes the bike to start free-wheeling down the slope, as the gravitational potential energy is changed into kinetic energy.

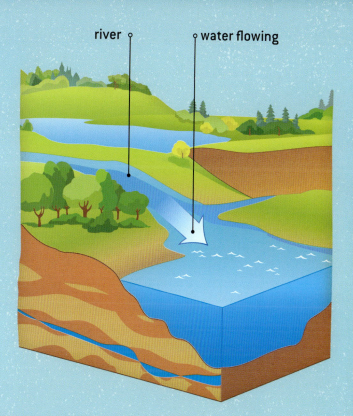

river · water flowing

▶ **What do you know about rivers, and the direction they flow?**

▶ **Can you think of a piece of technology that makes use of water and gravitational potential energy?**

 # CAN YOU SOLVE IT?

Consider the questions in each of the sections.

Think about what you already know about how electricity is generated – you might have seen some of the solutions in real life.

▶ Write down what you think the answers are, along with little sketches showing how they work.

Need some help? See page 42 for some solutions.

TEST IT!
BUILD A MINI WIND TURBINE

Convert kinetic energy from the wind into electricity using your own DIY miniature wind turbine.

YOU WILL NEED

a small hobby motor (available from electrical stores or online)

a plastic bottle

scissors

a 5-mm LED (available from electrical stores or online)

a hammer and nail

plasticine

a block of polystyrene or small cardboard box

tape

STEP ①

Cut the top off your plastic bottle from where the neck starts to curve. This part will make your fan blades (the turbine). Cut individual blades that are roughly three centimetres across by snipping inwards from the rim to where the lid screws on.

STEP ②

Bend the turbine blades backwards to make a flat circle, then twist each blade so they sit slightly at an angle.

STEP ③

Ask an adult for help making a small hole in the centre of the bottle's lid, the size of your hobby motor's axle. This can be done by gently tapping the tip of a nail into the plastic lid using the hammer.

STEP ④

Screw the lid onto the turbine, and slot it onto the axle of the hobby motor. If the axle is slightly smaller than the hole, secure it in place using plasticine.

STEP ⑤

Attach the LED to the back of the hobby motor by twisting each leg of the LED through one of the terminals that poke out the back of the motor. The LED will only work if the legs are connected to the correct terminals, so if the LED doesn't light up when the turbine is spinning, try switching the LED legs around.

STEP ⑥

Tape your motor to the top of the box or polystyrene block, so that the blades can spin freely. Try blowing on your turbine blades or holding it up to a fan to mimic the wind. Does your LED light up?

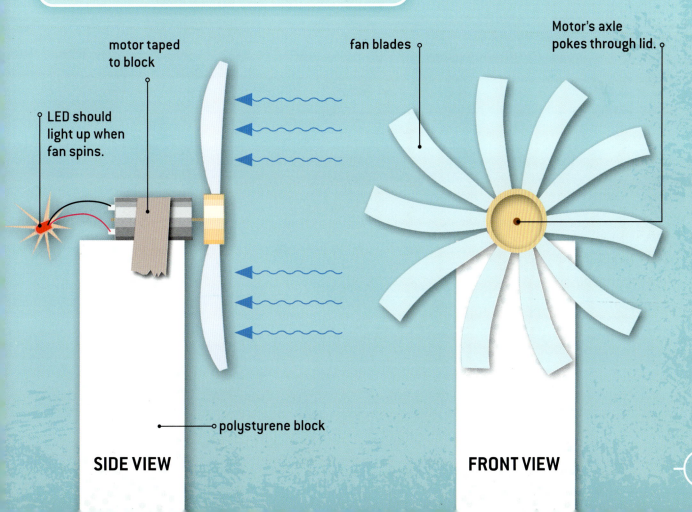

motor taped to block

LED should light up when fan spins.

fan blades

Motor's axle pokes through lid.

polystyrene block

SIDE VIEW

FRONT VIEW

THE ISSUE:
RUNNING OUT OF OIL

Coal, natural gas and crude oil are non-renewable resources. Aside from the damage they cause to our climate, a further problem is what will happen when they run out. Fossil fuels take millions of years to form, so it is essential to develop new energy systems that we will always be able to rely on.

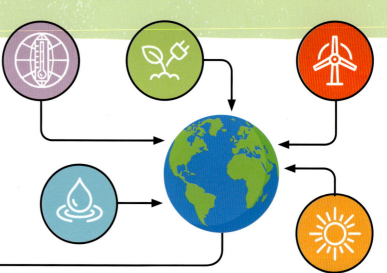

SPOTLIGHT:
RENEWABLE ENERGY

Sunlight, the wind, underground heat, biomass and moving water are all sources of renewable energy. This means they will never run out.

Deep down

Fossil fuels are mostly found deep underground. This means that getting them to the surface is not an easy and straightforward process. Wells that are thousands of metres deep need to be dug to extract oil. As we use up oil reserves closer to the surface, the wells need to be made deeper and deeper.

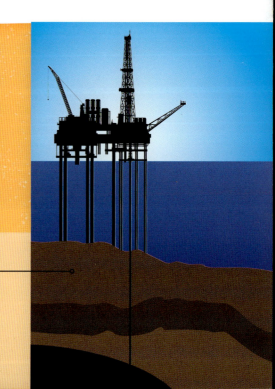

Oil platforms in the ocean are highly technical pieces of engineering. Some are built on huge towers that rest on the ocean floor. Others float on the surface, held in place by cables.

Ecosystem damage

Demand for oil is prompting oil companies to look in increasingly inaccessible places, such as the bottom of the oceans, and in pristine environments, such as the Arctic and tropical rainforests. Drilling and mining are seriously damaging to natural ecosystems, as the huge machinery rips up fragile habitats. Accidents such as oil spills also have devastating impacts on wildlife.

An oil pipeline runs through the Arctic tundra in Alaska, USA.

The Deepwater Horizon oil spill in the Gulf of Mexico released around 210 million gallons of oil into the ocean, killing thousands of marine birds and animals, and causing long-term environmental damage.

Beyond fuel

Oil is burned in power plants and refined into petrol, kerosene and other fuels for vehicles, but energy is only one thing it is used for. Oil is the raw material for plastic, as well as for a huge array of chemicals that we use in paints, medicines and as fertilisers in farming. Look around you right now, and many of the objects and materials you can see will be made from oil one way or another — and so developing alternatives will be essential once oil is no longer available.

ALTERNATIVE FUELS

Most of the energy on Earth ultimately comes from the Sun. Plants that grew millions of years ago using the process of photosynthesis to capture the Sun's energy eventually became today's fossil fuels. But plants growing right now also contain energy captured from the Sun, and these too are used as fuels.

Types of biofuel

Just as there are several types of fossil-based fuels used for different types of engine, such as petrol, diesel and kerosene, biofuels come in various types. Vegetable oil from soya beans can be burned directly as fuel in some engines or processed into biodiesel suitable for regular diesel engines. Strong alcohols made from wheat, corn or sugar can also be used as fuel.

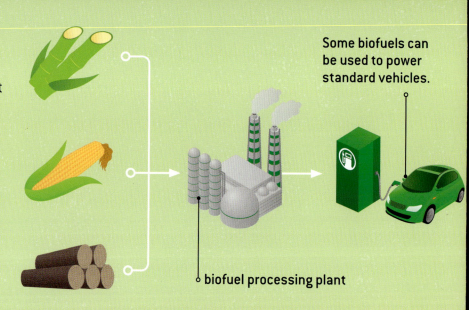

Some biofuels can be used to power standard vehicles.

biofuel processing plant

Biofuel benefits

The greatest advantage that biofuels have over fossil fuels is that they are a renewable resource. Crops can be grown and processed in a matter of months, rather than over millions of years. Plants can also be turned into alternative plastics and chemicals, called bioplastics and biochemicals.

Soya beans can be grown, harvested and processed within a year.

Problems with biofuel

Unfortunately, biofuels are not a 'magic bullet' solution to climate change. Despite the fact that burning them doesn't release carbon that has been stored in the ground for millions of years, growing the crops that make them does release carbon dioxide. Agriculture is a large source of carbon emissions, as ploughing soil and powering farm machinery such as tractors both emit greenhouse gases into the atmosphere.

Not enough space

Another problem with biofuels is the amount of land needed to grow them. Clearing forests and natural vegetation to grow the crops that make them destroys wildlife habitats and causes biodiversity loss. Because biofuels can be more profitable to grow than food crops, land that could be used to grow food is also often turned over to fuel production. This can mean that not enough food is grown to feed local people, particularly in poorer countries.

Growing enough soya beans to meet just the petrol and diesel fuel demands of the USA would require a land area **150%** larger than the size of the USA itself.

SOLVE IT!
SUSTAINABLE BIOFUEL

Biofuels that are made from purpose-grown crops are not a perfect alternative to our dependence on fossil fuels, due to the amount of land needed to grow them and the emissions released during farming. However, some biofuels can be produced that generate environmental benefits without the additional negative impacts. Can you see how?

FACT ONE

When organic matter such as food waste or animal manure is broken down by bacteria without oxygen present, it creates methane.

FACT TWO

Methane is a very powerful greenhouse gas that traps even more of the Sun's heat than CO_2 does.

heat from the Sun

atmosphere containing methane

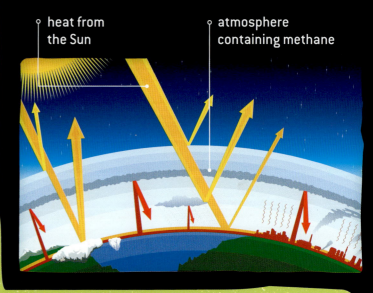

FACT THREE

Landfill sites (rubbish dumps) also give off a lot of methane, as the waste rots down.

FACT FOUR

Methane can be burnt as a fuel, like natural gas. It can power gas stoves for cooking, heating systems and vehicles. When methane is burnt, it produces carbon dioxide and water.

FACT FIVE

As well as producing methane, organic matter that is broken down by bacteria creates a sludge called 'digestate'. Digestate is full of the nutrients that plants need to grow.

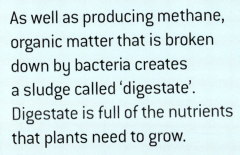

FACT SIX

One of the biggest problems with many biofuels is that land is given over to growing the fuel crops, when the land could be used for producing food, or as a habitat for wildlife.

 # CAN YOU SOLVE IT?

Look at the facts listed here. Can you think of a way to produce methane (or biogas) that doesn't take land away from food production or natural habitats?

▶ Can you see any other additional benefits to producing fuel from waste, aside from reducing our reliance on fossil fuels?

▶ Write down your ideas, and what you think the advantages are.

Still a bit stuck? See page 43 for the answer.

TEST IT!
MAKE BIOGAS

Brew up some biogas from food 'waste' with this experiment. Which types of waste produce the most gas? Caution: don't use sharp knives without permission, and remember methane is a flammable gas so keep this experiment away from open flames.

YOU WILL NEED

four uninflated balloons

four 500-ml plastic bottles

duct tape

a funnel

200 g mashed banana

200 g lettuce

200 g food scraps, left over from cooking

a fork and bowl

a teaspoon

a sharp knife and chopping board

kitchen scales

warm water

measuring tape

STEP ①

Weigh out 200 g of lettuce, and chop it very finely with the knife. Ask an adult for help chopping if you need to. Put the 200 g chopped lettuce into the first bottle.

STEP ②

Weigh out 200 g of banana, and mash it with a fork into a smooth puree. Spoon the 200 g of banana into the second bottle using the funnel.

STEP ③

Weigh 200 g of food scraps – these could be leftover vegetable peelings or uneaten food from your dinner. Chop or mash it into small pieces, and put it into the third bottle.

STEP ④

Fill up each of the bottles with warm water, taking care not to let them overflow. The fourth bottle will contain warm water only: this bottle will act as your control.

STEP ⑤

Stretch an uninflated balloon around the neck of each bottle. Secure the balloons in place with duct tape to ensure no air can leak.

STEP ⑥

Place your bottles in a warm spot such as a windowsill, away from any flames. Leave them for a few days.

STEP ⑦

After about a week, some of the balloons should have inflated with methane gas. Which has inflated the most? Wrap the measuring tape around the fattest part of each balloon to see which bottle has produced the most gas.

LETTUCE

BANANA

SCRAPS

CONTROL

Seal the balloons well with tape.

! CAUTION
Methane gas is flamable. Keep your bottles away from flames.

THE ISSUE:

POLLUTION IN THE AIR

Greenhouse gases such as carbon dioxide and methane are bad news for the atmosphere, but they aren't the only harmful substances produced by burning fossil fuels. Other gases and particles are also released into the air, with negative effects on people and the environment.

Toxic gases

Fossil fuels are primarily made of the elements carbon and hydrogen. However, they also contain small amounts of other elements, such as sulphur. When burned, the sulphur joins with oxygen in the air to make sulphur dioxide, a toxic gas. Burning fossil fuels without enough oxygen being present can also create carbon monoxide – another toxic gas – as well as soot (very small particles of carbon). Read more about how this works on the next page.

Polluted cities

Air pollution is a particularly big issue in cities, partly due to the amount of fossil fuels such as diesel and petrol being burnt in vehicle engines. In China, coal is used to fuel many power stations, which produces very high levels of soot. In cities such as Beijing, pollution from coal-fired power plants and vehicle engines create smog so thick it can even block out sunlight.

Beijing shrouded in thick smog

When air pollutants such as sulphur oxides and soot react with sunlight, it can create smog. This is visible air pollution that causes serious breathing difficulties. It is made worse by certain weather patterns that trap smoggy air close to the ground.

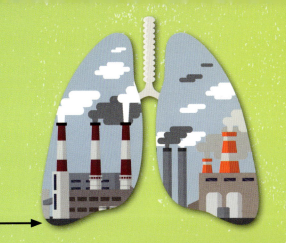

Human health

Air containing toxic gases such as sulphur dioxide, carbon monoxide and other pollutants such as soot can be very harmful to human health. Breathing polluted air damages the lungs, triggers asthma and is linked to other problems such as stroke and heart disease.

A man in China wears a face mask to protect against pollution.

Air pollution causes around 6.5 million premature deaths each year around the world.

Environmental damage

Sulphur dioxide and nitrogen oxide (another chemical released by burning fossil fuels in car engines) mix with water in the atmosphere, making it acidic. This acidic water then falls as acid rain. Acid rain is very harmful to plants and animals, especially aquatic creatures such as fish and amphibians.

The trees in this German forest have died due to acid rain.

WHAT HAPPENS WHEN FUELS BURN?

How exactly does burning fossil fuels release carbon dioxide and other pollutants into the air? It's all to do with the chemical reaction called combustion (the scientific word for 'burning').

Atoms and elements

Everything in the world is made from atoms – the unimaginably tiny building blocks of stuff. There are over 100 different types of atom that scientists have already discovered, which we call elements. Carbon is an element, as are oxygen, gold and iron. Some materials are made up of just one type of element: a piece of solid gold, for example, contains only gold atoms. But most materials contain a mixture of elements.

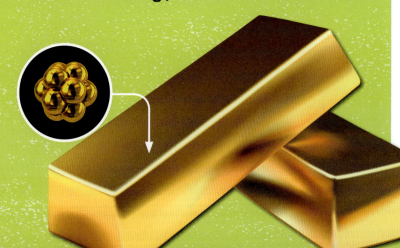

Pure gold is an element, made from one type of atom.

Compounds and energy

A material made from more than one element joined together is called a compound. Water is made of hydrogen and oxygen, which is why its scientific name is dihydrogen oxide, or H_2O. Water and carbon dioxide are both examples of compounds. The smallest 'piece' a compound comes in is a molecule. A molecule is made when a group of atoms have joined very tightly, or 'bonded' together. It takes energy to make these bonds, and energy to break them, too.

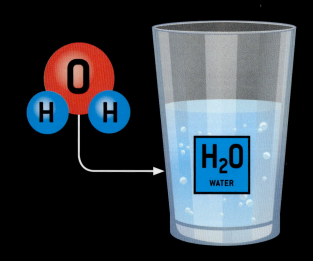

A chemical reaction

Burning, or combustion, is a type of chemical reaction. Fossil fuels are mostly made from the elements hydrogen and carbon tightly bonded together. But adding heat to these fuels in the presence of oxygen causes the chemical reaction of combustion. The bonds between the hydrogen and carbon atoms are broken, and they form new bonds with the oxygen in the air, creating new CO_2 molecules and new H_2O molecules.

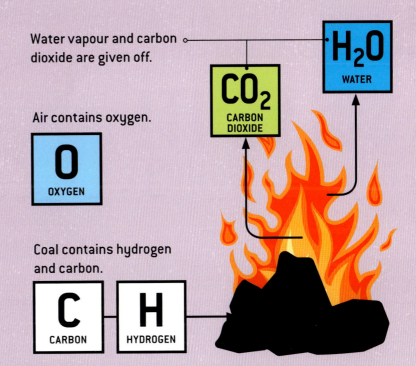

Water vapour and carbon dioxide are given off.

H₂O WATER

CO₂ CARBON DIOXIDE

Air contains oxygen.

O OXYGEN

Coal contains hydrogen and carbon.

C CARBON **H** HYDROGEN

Giving off energy

There is a lot of energy in the bonds that join the hydrogen and carbon atoms together in fossil fuels. As the bonds break during combustion, the energy that was stored up in them is given off as heat and light energy.

Incomplete combustion

Soot and the toxic gas carbon monoxide (CO) are given off when fuel is burned without enough oxygen present, and there aren't enough oxygen atoms to go round. Carbon dioxide (CO_2) has two oxygen atoms for each carbon atom, but carbon monoxide (CO) has only one. Tiny bits of carbon are also left over – this is what soot is.

SOLVE IT!
POWER A VEHICLE

Huge amounts of greenhouse gases and air pollution are released into the atmosphere by our cars, ships and planes. How could we power the vehicles we use without creating air pollution? Come up with some solutions to this challenge using the information below.

FACT ONE

Electric vehicles are already available. Instead of having an engine that burns fossil fuels, they are powered by batteries.

FACT TWO

Electric vehicles work by charging up their batteries from a mains source of electricity. This is electricity that is generated elsewhere and carried to the car's charging point by cables.

FACT THREE

30 per cent of car journeys made by people in Europe cover distances of less than three kilometres. 50 per cent are less than five kilometres.

FACT FOUR

Photovoltaic cells, also called solar cells, are a type of technology that can generate electricity directly from sunlight.

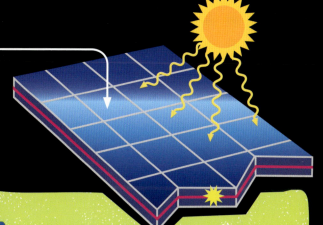

FACT FIVE

Photovoltaic cells need quite a lot of surface area to capture sunlight, but they are very light, and can even be made into a transparent film.

CAN YOU SOLVE IT?

Thinking about the pieces of information listed here, can you think of THREE different ways that we can reduce the amount of greenhouse gases and air pollution produced by our transport?

▶ What types of vehicle already exist
  – do they all need to burn fuels?

▶ Where does our mains electricity come from
  – does it have to create greenhouse gases?

▶ Could we design an entirely new way of powering cars and other vehicles?

▶ How else can we reduce vehicle emissions?

Need some inspiration? See page 44 for some ideas.

TEST IT!
SOLAR-POWERED MINI CAR

Create your own tiny eco-friendly vehicle with this project.

YOU WILL NEED

- a small hobby motor with pulley
- a solar cell with wires (cell and motor available online or from electrical stores)
- a large rubber band
- two A4 pieces of thick cardboard
- two long wooden skewers
- two non-bendy drinking straws
- scissors
- sticky tape
- PVA glue
- a pair of compasses and a pencil

STEP ①

Using the compasses, draw two small wheels and two large wheels on one sheet of cardboard. Draw a fifth wheel that is a few milimetres smaller in diameter than the large wheels. Cut them out, and poke very small holes in the centre of each using a skewer.

STEP ②

Stack the two large wheels with the slightly smaller wheel in the middle. Check to see if your rubber band will fit easily in the groove created between the two large wheels. You may need to add an additional small wheel in between to make the groove wider. When the band fits, glue the wheels together to create a single pulley wheel.

STEP ③

Cut down your second sheet of cardboard so that it is about the same width as your drinking straws. Tape one drinking straw near the back and on the underside of your cardboard.

STEP ④

Cut a slit in the middle of your cardboard, near the front. It should be slightly wider and a bit longer than your pulley wheel. Cut your second drinking straw in half, and tape the two halves either side of the slit.

STEP ⑤

Loop one end of the rubber band around your pulley wheel. Loop the other end around the pulley on the motor.

STEP ⑥

Put the pulley wheel with band around into the slit in the cardboard, and thread one skewer through the pieces of straw and the centre of the pulley wheel.

STEP ⑦

Tape the motor onto the top of the cardboard behind the wheel so the rubber band is taut. Attach the wires from the solar cell to the terminals on the motor, and tape the solar cell behind the motor.

STEP ⑧

Slide a skewer through the rear straw, and slot a small cardboard wheel onto each end of it. Your mini car is ready: test it out in bright sunshine!

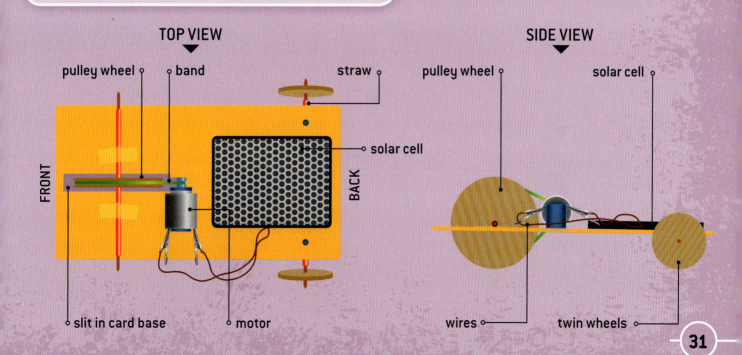

TOP VIEW ▼

pulley wheel   band   straw

FRONT   solar cell   BACK

slit in card base   motor

SIDE VIEW ▼

pulley wheel   solar cell

wires   twin wheels

THE ISSUE:
WASTED ENERGY

The majority of our electricity is generated in large, fossil fuel powered plants. These are connected to homes and businesses by a network of cables and power lines called the grid. Unfortunately, the way that electricity is currently generated and transported is not very efficient, so a lot of energy is wasted.

Energy demand

We use a lot of electricity, but not at a steady rate. The amount of electricity being used by people and businesses at any one time is called the energy demand. Demand for electricity is very high at certain points during the day, but very low at night when people are asleep. But because our power stations take a long time to get up and running, they are kept on during times of low demand, unnecessarily burning fuel and producing greenhouse gases.

A power station in Hong Kong at night

SPOTLIGHT: TV PICKUP

In the UK, 'TV pickup' is an effect where demand for electricity surges at certain moments during very widely watched TV programes, such as the football World Cup. Large numbers of people take advantage of breaks to get up and boil the kettle or collect food or drinks from fridges, causing a spike in national electricity use!

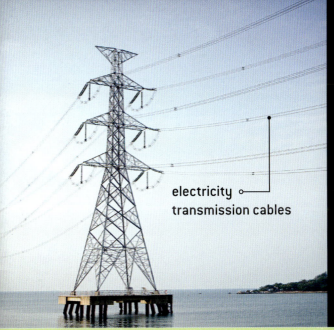

electricity transmission cables

Lost in transmission

Have you ever heard a power line crackling? That's because electricity cables can't conduct a perfect 100 per cent of electricity. Some energy is lost along the way as heat or sound. In many countries around the world, poor quality or ageing cables and network technology cause high energy losses during transmission, wasting power before it reaches homes and businesses.

In Togo in Africa,
73%
of electricity generated gets lost during transmission. In Singapore, the loss is only 2 per cent.

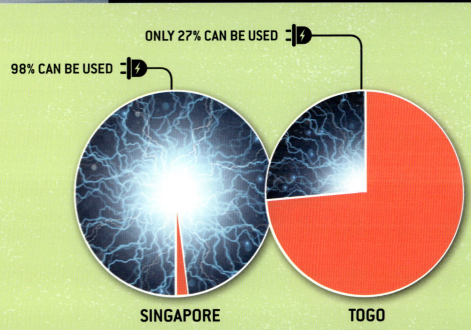

98% CAN BE USED

ONLY 27% CAN BE USED

SINGAPORE

TOGO

Intermittent power

Renewable sources such as wind and solar avoid the problem of unnecessary greenhouse gas emissions generated when electricity demand is low, but they have their own technological challenges. One is that the wind isn't always blowing, and the Sun isn't always shining! This is called 'intermittency'. Finding ways to store energy from the Sun and wind and release it when needed is an important part of building a reliable energy network. Read more about this on the next page.

daytime

nighttime

UNDERSTANDING ELECTRICITY

Electricity is the movement of electrical charge. Electrical charge is carried by electrons, and so the movement of electrons is what creates an electrical current that can power our devices.

Parts of an atom

Atoms, the world's tiny building blocks, are themselves made up of even smaller bits called neutrons, protons and electrons. The exact number of protons and electrons in an atom is what determines the type of element it is. Protons and neutrons clump together at the centre of an atom, but the tiny electrons whizz around the edges.

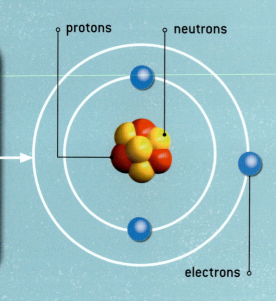

protons   neutrons

electrons

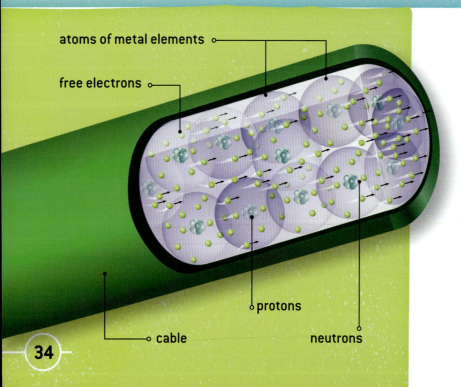

atoms of metal elements

free electrons

protons

cable   neutrons

Flowing electrons

Because electrons are on the outside of the atom, they are more easily separated from the rest. They can jump from one atom to the next. Conductors are materials that swap electrons like this very easily. As electrons flow through an electrical device, they make it work, a little like how a stream of water can flow through a water wheel and make it turn.

Battery technology

Electricity needs to be flowing in order to do work, just as still water won't power a water wheel. However, sometimes we need to be able to store energy for later use, such as in networks containing wind and solar power plants. Rechargeable batteries do this by converting electrical energy to chemical energy, then back again when it needs to be used.

Mobile phones have rechargeable batteries.

SPOTLIGHT: LITHIUM ION BATTERIES

One of the lightest and most efficient types of battery technology we have at the moment is the lithium ion battery. These batteries are used in electric vehicles, and to store energy from renewable power generators such as solar panels and windmills.

Disadvantages of batteries

Lithium ion and similar chemical batteries are incredibly useful, but they do have downsides. As more people choose electric cars, and new renewable power plants are built, the demand for these sorts of batteries will go up. But lithium and other similar metals are finite resources, which have to be mined from underground and processed using toxic chemicals. This can cause pollution and damage natural habitats. They are also expensive to produce, and lose efficiency over time.

A lithium mine in Australia

SOLVE IT!
STORE THE SUN'S ENERGY

In order to make best use of renewable sources such as the Sun we need to be able to store energy, as well as generating electricity for immediate use. Can you use the facts below to figure out one solution for storing the Sun's energy?

FACT ONE

Photovoltaic (solar) panels immediately convert light energy from the Sun into electrical energy, but they only work when the Sun is shining.

FACT TWO

As well as light energy, the Sun gives off heat energy. This heat energy can be concentrated and focused on a small area using mirrors.

FACT THREE

Concentrated heat from the Sun can heat materials to very high temperatures.

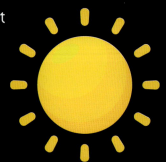

FACT FOUR

Some types of salt turn into liquid when they are heated to high temperatures. This hot liquid can be pumped around or stored as needed.

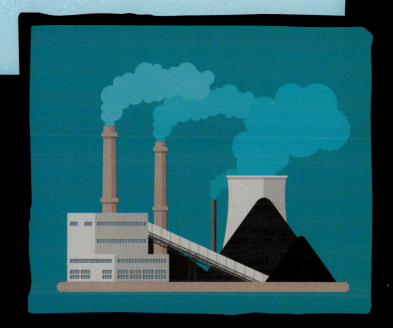

FACT FIVE

Heat energy is an important part of producing electricity in standard fossil fuel powered plants (see pages 10–11).

 CAN YOU SOLVE IT?

Heat is a type of energy that can be used during electricity generation. Thinking about the facts above, how could you collect heat from the Sun, and use it as needed to produce electricity? Think about:

► How we make electricity in traditional fossil fuel plants.

► How the different elements mentioned here could be connected together.

► Try drawing a diagram of your idea.

Feeling confused? Turn to page 45!

TEST IT!
MAKE A SOLAR OVEN

Warm up some food and explore the power of the Sun's heat when focused by reflective surfaces by making your own solar oven.

YOU WILL NEED

a cardboard box, such as a shoebox, with an attached lid

aluminium foil

glue

cling film

sticky tape

a long wooden skewer

a craft knife

some food for melting, such as wraps with grated cheese or biscuits with pieces of chocolate on top

STEP ①

Ask an adult to help you cut a flap out of the lid of the box using the craft knife. You want to create a large flap that attaches to the box on one side. Leave a 3 cm border around the edge of the flap.

cut

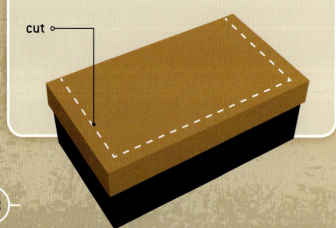

STEP ②

Line the entire inside of the box with aluminium foil, including the underside of the flap you have just created. Glue the foil in place, making sure the dull side is the side that is glued, and the foil is as smooth and flat as possible.

STEP ③

With the flap lifted open, cover the opening completely with two layers of cling film. Tape one layer to the underside of the lid, and one to the top, creating a narrow gap between the two layers.

STEP ④

Use the skewer to prop the flap open, and set the box in direct sunshine to pre-heat for around half an hour. Angle the box so it is catching as much sunlight as possible.

STEP ⑤

After about half an hour, lift up the cling film lid and place your wrap with grated cheese, or biscuit with chocolate pieces inside your solar oven. Close the cling film lid, but keep the foil flap propped open with the skewer to reflect sunlight into the oven.

STEP ⑥

Leave your food in the oven until it is all melty and warm. This should take around 30 to 60 minutes depending on the strength of the Sun. When it is ready, take it out and enjoy!

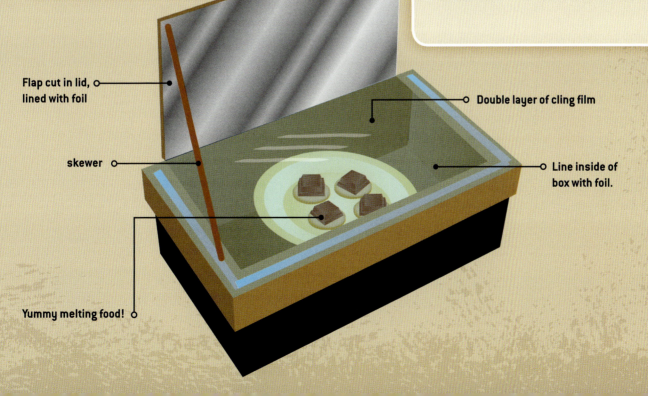

Flap cut in lid, lined with foil

skewer

Yummy melting food!

Double layer of cling film

Line inside of box with foil.

THE FUTURE OF POWER

The urgent need to move away from relying on fossil fuels is motivating scientists and engineers to work on hundreds of different solutions for how to meet our energy needs. Some alternatives are already well-established science facts, while others are still closer to science fiction! Here are just a few futuristic ideas for energy technology.

A nuclear power plant in Dukovany, Czech Republic

New nuclear

Nuclear power has been around for decades, but currently it is based on fission. This means the energy is produced when atoms are split apart. Although nuclear fission doesn't produce greenhouse gases, it does produce a lot of dangerous radioactive waste. This waste remains harmful for thousands of years. Scientists are trying to develop a type of nuclear power based on fusion – or joining atoms together – instead. Unlike fission, fusion doesn't create dangerous radioactive waste. Unfortunately, so far, no one has been able to make nuclear fusion work on a big enough scale to produce power.

SPOTLIGHT: NUCLEAR FUSION

Fusion is the same type of reaction that is going on inside the Sun. Two hydrogen atoms are fused together to create a single helium atom.

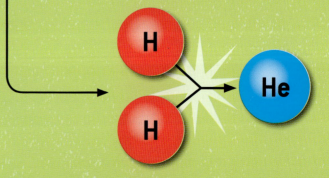

Space solar

There's one place that the Sun is always shining — in space! Space-based solar power is the idea of collecting solar energy in space, converting it into microwaves (a type of radiation similar to radio waves), and beaming it down to Earth. Large satellite dishes would collect the microwaves on the Earth's surface, and convert them to electrical energy.

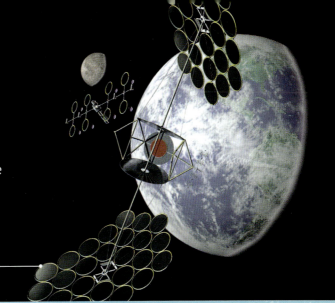

A concept for a solar power collector in space designed by NASA

Global supergrid

Another way to address the problem of intermittency (see page 33) is to connect renewable power stations all around the world in a giant grid. After all, it's always sunny or windy somewhere in the world! This idea of connecting lots of power plants could be used on a smaller scale too. If every community nationwide had solar panels or a wind turbine, we wouldn't need to rely on large, centralised power plants. Instead, electricity would be being generated in small amounts up and down the country, and shared by everyone on the grid.

At current levels of efficiency, we could meet the world's electricity needs with solar panels covering an area of

496,805 SQ KM

or approximately the size of Spain.

Scientists and engineers around the globe are developing many kinds of new technology to harness renewable energy sources. Here are some key renewable technologies:

WIND

Moving air contains kinetic energy. It can be used to spin the blades of a wind turbine, which is connected to a generator by gears that increase the speed of the spinning motion.

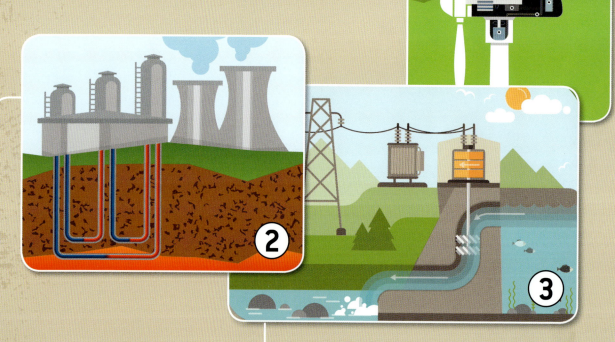

EARTH

In volcanic areas where the Earth's heat is near the surface, pipes can be drilled into the ground. Water can be pumped through the pipes and boiled by the heat of the surrounding rocks, creating steam to drive generators. This is called geothermal energy.

WATER

When water falls onto high ground, it collects into rivers and flows downwards towards the sea, pulled by gravity. A dam is a way of holding river water back, collecting gravitational potential energy. Small channels in the dam wall contain turbines that are spun very fast as water flows through them. The gravitational potential energy is converted to kinetic energy.

Biogas, or methane, can be made from waste instead of purpose-grown crops. There are a couple of different ways of generating or collecting biogas:

animal manure

Food waste from people's homes and animal manure from farms can be collected and taken to processing plants to be turned into biogas and digestate (see page 21).

food waste

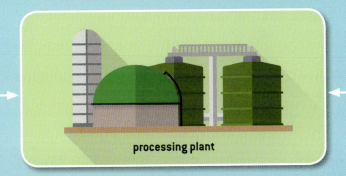

processing plant

covered landfill site

Landfill sites can be covered, and as the methane rises to the surface it can be collected and piped off.

methane storage tanks

Apart from providing energy, using the methane that is produced by landfills and from animal and food waste as energy has an additional advantage. Methane is much more powerful as a greenhouse gas than carbon dioxide. Burning methane converts it into the less powerful greenhouse gases carbon dioxide and water vapour.

Digestate can also be used as a fertiliser for food crops, replacing fertilisers made from fossil fuels.

ANSWERS

There are a number of ways we can reduce the amount of greenhouse gases and air pollution released into the atmosphere as a result of our vehicles. Here are three ideas:

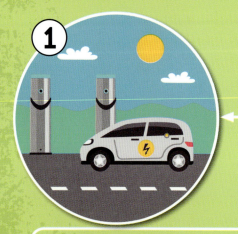

① Electric vehicles

We can replace our petrol and diesel cars with electric vehicles. However, in order to make these truly eco-friendly, the electricity that is used to charge their batteries would need to be generated by renewable means.

Walking and cycling

A lot of journeys are made by car when they don't need to be. We can reduce emissions straight away by choosing to walk or cycle where possible, instead of driving.

② Solar vehicles

③ Scientists are working on creating vehicles that are covered in solar panels, which could generate their own electricity as they went along! An aeroplane called Solar Impulse has already circumnavigated the globe. It has very wide wings covered in solar cells, and is designed to be as light as possible to save energy. At the moment Solar Impulse can only carry one person, but improvements in technology could make solar vehicles viable in the future.

'Thermal energy storage' is the name for a variety of technologies that store heat energy to be used later. There are several different types of heat storage technology, but one is molten-salt technology, and it works like this:

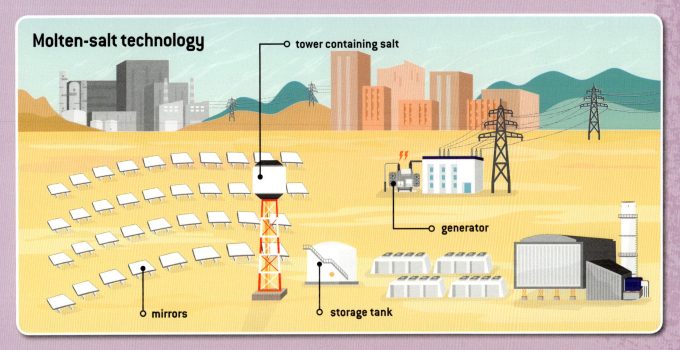

Molten-salt technology

- tower containing salt
- generator
- mirrors
- storage tank

Specially angled mirrors reflect the Sun to a central tower, concentrating the heating power into a small area. In the tower, salt is heated to 566°C. In its molten, liquid state it is pumped to insulated storage tanks that keep it hot for many hours, even up to a week. When the energy is needed, the hot salt is used to boil water, which drives a standard steam turbine and generator.

Home heating

Aside from large power plants that capture the Sun's heat to generate electricity, a simpler technology that uses solar thermal energy has been in use for a long time. Panels filled with thin water pipes can be installed on the roofs of buildings. The Sun heats the water in the pipes, which can then be used to provide hot water or heating for the building.

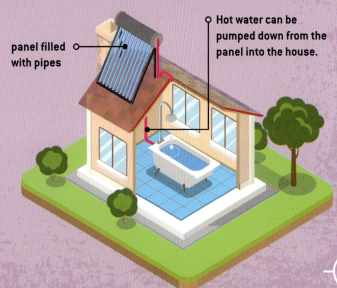

- panel filled with pipes
- Hot water can be pumped down from the panel into the house.

MAKING A DIFFERENCE

We all use energy every day, when we use our electrical devices and take transport. We also indirectly use energy through the food we eat and the things we buy, as these are produced using energy. We can all help to reduce the amount of greenhouse gases and air pollution created by our energy use by making some simple changes.

Don't waste energy

Turn off lights and other electrical devices when they are not in use. Dry laundry on a rack, rather than in the tumble dryer. Wear an extra layer instead of turning up the heating at home.

Avoid being driven to places by car if you can help it – walk or cycle instead. Try and buy food and other items that are made locally too, instead of products that have been transported thousands of miles to reach you.

Go renewable

Ask around at home to find out which company supplies your electricity. There are many energy companies that generate all of their electricity through renewable means, and by getting your family to switch to one of these you can make a big difference to how much CO_2 your family is responsible for.

GLOSSARY

acid rain rainfall made acidic by pollution that has been released into the atmosphere from factories

atom the tiny building blocks that make up everything in the universe

biodiversity the variety of living things found in a particular area

biofuel fuel made from plants that have just been harvested, instead of plants and animals that have been underground for millions of years

biogas a type of fuel gas that is made from plants or from rubbish

biomass organic material such as wood, straw or animal dung that can be burned and used as an energy source

chemical energy energy stored in the bonds between atoms inside molecules

climate change the changes in world weather patterns caused by human activity

combustion a chemical reaction that produces heat and light; the scientific name for burning

compound a material that is made of more than one element, chemically bonded together

digestate the material that is left behind when waste or plants are made into biofuel. It is used as fertiliser for crops

element a pure substance that is made from a single type of atom

fossil fuel a fuel such as oil or coal that was formed over millions of years from dead plants and animals

generator a machine that produces electricity

geothermal energy when the heat from inside the Earth is used to generate energy

global warming the heating of the Earth due to the greenhouse effect

greenhouse effect the way that the atmosphere traps heat from the Sun; made more powerful by gases such as carbon dioxide and methane

greenhouse gas a gas such as carbon dioxide or methane that when added to the atmosphere increases the greenhouse effect

grid the network of power plants and cables that deliver electricity to people in homes and factories

Industrial Revolution a period in world history when big changes happened in the way things were made and society was organised, with a focus on machines instead of doing things by hand

intermittency something that starts and stops, such as the wind or the sunshine that is used to generate renewable electricity

internal combustion engine an engine commonly used in vehicles that burns fuels such as petrol and diesel to produce kinetic energy

kinetic energy movement energy

molecule the smallest possible 'piece' of a material

nuclear fission the process of splitting a large atom into two or more smaller atoms, which releases a lot of energy

nuclear fusion the process of joining two or more small atoms into one larger atom, which releases a lot of energy

photovoltaic cell a device that turns the energy in sunlight directly into electrical energy

potential energy energy that is stored inside an object or material

renewable energy energy that has been generated from a source that will never run out, such as wind energy or solar energy

smog a fog containing pollution and smoke

sustainable when something can be maintained at the same level for a very long time because it doesn't harm the environment or use up limited natural resources

thermal energy storage a technology that allows the storage and transfer of heat energy

transmission the process of sending electricity from one place to another

turbine a machine that uses the kinetic energy in moving water or air to create a spinning motion, which can drive a generator or a mill

INDEX

ECO STEAM

TITLES IN THE SERIES

the CITIES WE LIVE IN

City life

Eco-freindly cities

THE ISSUE: Urban sprawl

Urban land use

Solve it! Sustainable city planning

Test it! Land use project

THE ISSUE: Lack of green space

Heating and cooling

Solve it! Cool the city

Test it! The albedo effect

THE ISSUE: Too much traffic

Transport technology

Solve it! Increase public transport

Test it! Weigh your car

THE ISSUE: Light pollution

Understanding light

Solve it! Reduce light pollution

Test it! Street light design

Cities in the future

the CROPS WE GROW

Farming around the world

Impacts of farming

THE ISSUE: Rainforest deforestation

Habitat destruction

Solve it! Farm without deforestation

Test it! Mixed-veg garden project

THE ISSUE: Soil erosion

What is soil?

Solve it! Protect the soil

Test it! Soil erosion experiment

THE ISSUE: Pollinators under threat

Plants, pollinators and ecosystems

Solve it! Pollinator-friendly farming

Test it! Pollinator survey

THE ISSUE: Lost plant variety

Evolution and inheritance

Solve it! Climate-proof farming

Test it! Heritage varieties

Farming in the future

the ENERGY WE USE

Understanding energy

How we use fuels

THE ISSUE: Climate change

Producing power

Solve it! Green energy sources

Test it! Build a mini-wind turbine

THE ISSUE: Running out of oil

Alternative fuels

Solve it! Fuel from waste

Test it! Biogas experiment

THE ISSUE: Pollution in the air

What happens when fuels burn?

Solve it! Power a vehicle

Test it! Make a mini-solar car

THE ISSUE: Energy demand

Battery technology

Solve it! 24 hour-power

Test it! Solar heater experiment

The future of power

the FOOD WE EAT

Food, waste and climate change

The big issues

THE ISSUE: Animal farming impacts

Diet and nutrition

Solve it! Design a balanced menu

Test it! Make bean burgers

THE ISSUE: Overfishing

Food chains and ecosystems

Solve it! Sustainable fish farming

Test it! Grow lettuces in water

THE ISSUE: Problems with packaging

Properties of plastics

Solve it! Preventing plastic pollution

Test it! Make corn plastic

THE ISSUE: Food waste

Decomposition

Solve it! Waste-free sugar

Test it! Make your own compost

Food in the futureIndex

the HOUSES WE BUILD

The technology of building

Impacts of construction

THE ISSUE: A concrete problem

Sustainable materials

Solve it! Design eco-homes

Test it! Make a brick

THE ISSUE: Energy-hungry homes

The Earth's tilt

Solve it! Using the Sun's energy

Test it! Sunlight and the seasons

THE ISSUE: Too hot or too cold

Thermal energy transfers

Solve it! Prevent heat loss

Test it! Insulation experiment

THE ISSUE: Unsustainable water use

The water cycle

Solve it! Reduce water consumption

Test it! Make a water filter

Houses in the future

the STUFF WE BUY

Material World

Making things, making waste

THE ISSUE: Throwaway fashion

How fabric is made

Solve It! Cotton alternatives

Test it! Upcycled clothing

THE ISSUE: Polluting paper

Product manufacturing

Solve it! Stop wasting resources

Test it! Handmade paper

THE ISSUE: Waste electronics

What is circular design?

Solve it! A new system

Test it! Make a toy

THE ISSUE: Too much stuff

How we use things

Solve it! Saving and sharing

Test it! Build a sharing website

The future of making